Dyin

Elound

A LION POCKETBOOK

Text copyright © 1990 Elizabeth Round
This edition copyright © 1990 Lion Publishing
Illustrations copyright © 1990 Pat Gregory

Published by
Lion Publishing
850 North Grove Avenue, Elgin, Illinois 60120, USA
ISBN 0 7459 1952 9
Lion Publishing plc
Sandy Lane West, Oxford, England
ISBN 0 7459 1952 9
Albatross Books Pty Ltd
PO Box 320, Sutherland, NSW 2232, Australia
ISBN 0 7324 0244 1

First edition 1990
10 9 8 7 6 5 4 3 2 1

Printed and bound in Slovenia

Contents

1
Hooked on Dieting

Sandra, now twenty-eight, started to develop an eating disorder when she was sixteen. With hindsight, she believes a number of factors led to the problem. 'I was making the transition from childhood to adolescence and not coping well with it. I was frightened of growing up, nervous of men, a very protected child and a perfectionist.'

Her desire for a 'perfect' figure prompted her to go on a diet following a summer holiday. 'Slowly but steadily, the obsession with what I ate and weighed became focal in my life,' she recalls. Physical weight loss was not immediately apparent, but her family and friends noticed other changes—Sandra no longer ate with other people; she never wore a skirt or dress; and she buried herself in her studies, becoming 'very serious about everything'.

Her diet continued after she went to college to study languages. She weighed herself three or four

'If I ever felt I had overdone the eating, the only way to feel good again was to burn off the calories.'

times every day, panicking if the scales showed any increase. She counted calories: 'In class I would often find myself jotting down totals on the back cover of my exercise book.' Although Sandra was hungry, she always denied it, not allowing herself to eat. 'I developed weird habits. I would pick off the edges of cakes and bread, and nibble them—almost as if I were desperate to eat but would not allow myself to do so.'

Sandra also became hooked on fitness routines as a means of getting rid of unwanted calories. 'I would jog early in the morning, do exercises in my room, swim miles. If I ever felt I had overdone the eating, the only way to feel good again was to burn off the calories.'

As her diet continued, Sandra became increasingly withdrawn. 'I was unaware of anyone else. I couldn't laugh, cry or feel for anyone or anything. Food and calories were my life.'

She remembers that as she lost weight, the rational part of her mind told her that her obsession was dangerous and that it should stop. 'But, although I sometimes promised myself I would stop dieting, I did not have the power to do so. I was in the grip of something totally destructive. It had a hold on me I could not break.' And, although her weight dropped to just five stone (seventy pounds), she could still look in a mirror and see herself as too fat. She became depressed, and felt 'very frightened, and very, very low'.

One morning, Sandra felt too weak to get out of bed. She was taken to hospital and put on an intravenous drip.

'Although I protested violently at the time, I now see how necessary it was for me to have been taken under someone else's wing,' Sandra reflects. 'I had reached a stage where I was out of control. In a matter of weeks, I would probably have been dead.'

2

The Eating Disorders

For most people in the Western world, eating is a
natural, essential and enjoyable part of everyday life.
But for an increasing number of women and teenage
girls, and a smaller number of men, food has become
something to be feared and, whenever possible,
avoided. They are obsessed with weight, calories and
food, to the virtual exclusion of everything else. They
suffer from eating disorders: anorexia nervosa,
bulimia nervosa and compulsive eating.

☐ Juliet, a 33-year-old teacher, eats only on alternate
days. She binges on food on her 'eating days' and
then takes laxatives to get rid of the food she has
eaten. She has been dieting and bingeing since she
was seventeen and feels guilty about the amount of
money she 'wastes' on food.

☐ Tina, a twenty-year-old student, starves herself
for weeks, eating only the occasional bowl of soup,

in order to keep her weight down. She likes being too thin. She is afraid to eat because she knows that, for her, the alternative to not eating is eating too much.

☐ Kate, a mother in her late thirties, has put on seven stone (ninety-eight pounds) in seven years, despite repeated efforts to diet and to control her over-eating. She is concerned about the effect her eating problems will have on her children.

Whether sufferers are overweight, underweight or average weight, they all share the same fears of food and weight gain. They all desire extreme thinness. And they are all unhappy with themselves and with life in general.

Many sufferers keep their eating problems secret, believing that they are the one person in the world with such a problem and that everyone else would be shocked and disgusted by their bizarre eating habits. This is not the case.

In the United States, some six million people are known to suffer from eating disorders. In the United Kingdom, there are around 140,000 registered anorexics and bulimics. These statistics refer only to reported cases; given the secrecy associated with eating disorders, and the fact that compulsive eating and bulimia are sometimes not treated seriously by the medical profession, the actual figures are likely to be much higher.

Sufferers are usually female—only one in ten is male. Although people between eight and eighty have been treated for an eating disorder, most sufferers of anorexia and bulimia are in their teens and early twenties.

So, if you are currently battling with an eating disorder, there is no need to feel isolated and 'freakish'. You are not alone.

3
Anorexia Nervosa

'The determination I need just to eat one meal!' says Alison. 'I live in fear of my body growing. I feel as if I want to hide away, as if the whole world is watching me. Food is everywhere I go. I see the food before I see the person who is eating it.'

Alison has anorexia nervosa, the best known of the eating disorders. The term means 'nervous loss of appetite', and it was identified as an emotional disorder as early as the seventeenth century. Many people associate anorexia nervosa with dieting, yet most anorexics have not lost their appetites and most dieters do not become anorexic.

Today the condition has become almost fashionable. Maybe this is partly because so many celebrities have been anorexic. The media and social pressures to be slim have made a near-anorexic figure desirable. In reality, anorexia is far from glamorous. It is a disease

However low her weight may drop, an anorexic will see herself as fat.

that makes people unattractive and unhealthy, and it can lead eventually to death.

Most anorexics do not know they have this condition. They know anorexia exists but do not think it applies to them.

How can you tell if you might be anorexic? If you are suffering from anorexia, you will:

☐ see yourself as hideously fat, though the scales tell you that you are underweight for your height;

☐ feel compelled to eat as little as possible and to exercise regularly in order to lose more weight;

☐ make yourself vomit, take laxatives, or exercise more if you eat more than your daily calorie 'allowance';

☐ find it increasingly difficult to concentrate on anything other than food, calories and your weight;

☐ weigh yourself several times a day and panic if the scales show a slight increase;

☐ spend hours studying recipe books and scanning supermarket shelves;

☐ enjoy cooking food for other people, while avoiding eating it yourself;

☐ become deceitful about your eating habits—skipping meals, making excuses, hiding or throwing away food;

☐ develop rituals, such as eating at exactly the same time every day, and panic if you can't adhere to them;

☐ become increasingly introverted, socially isolated and irritable.

Anorexia involves more than weight loss. Its physical effects include emaciation, abdominal pains, constipation, insomnia, poor circulation and low blood pressure. Menstrual periods cease, and hair loss may occur. In extreme cases, teeth fall out and downy hair appears on the body and face.

Despite this, most anorexics deny that they are losing weight, deny that there is anything wrong, and deny that they are ill. Anorexics are consumed with fear—fear of gaining weight, fear of losing control over food and their lives, and fear of getting better. Denial and fear keep people locked in anorexia.

The body can take only so much of this treatment. Many anorexics, unable to maintain their rigid control over eating, fall into another eating disorder, bulimia nervosa, purging their bodies of what they eat so they can eat what they like and remain thin. Some binge but do not purge, putting on vast amounts of weight. Some anorexics die of their disease or commit suicide.

Despite all this, many sufferers, with a genuine desire and determination to get better whatever the personal cost, recover. They are able to lead normal lives once more.

4
Bulimia Nervosa

'Six years ago I suffered from anorexia, but only for a year or so,' says Penny. 'I thought I was over it, but during the next few years I continued to be obsessed with food. Two years ago I became so desperate and suicidal that I agreed to outpatient treatment at the hospital. I was diagnosed as having bulimia nervosa.'

The term bulimia nervosa means 'nervous insatiable appetite'. It was identified in 1979, following a study of thirty patients by British doctor Gerald Russell. The patients had an irresistible urge to overeat, combined with an overwhelming fear of putting on weight. Because most of the patients had previously been anorexic, Dr Russell concluded that bulimia was an aftermath of anorexia.

Most bulimics have previously had, or been close to having, anorexia. The condition usually begins when a dieter discovers that she can eat what she likes and avoid later weight gain by making herself vomit or by taking massive quantities of laxatives or diuretics.

After bingeing and purging, she tries to regain control by starvation dieting—until the next binge occurs. The bulimic eventually finds herself bingeing more frequently, until she is bingeing and purging—always in secret—several times a day.

If you are suffering from bulimia, you will:

☐ binge on huge amounts of high-carbohydrate foods you normally would not allow yourself to eat. When a binge is full-blown, a bulimic will often eat anything; Penny turned to frozen food and dog food if there was nothing else around;

☐ eat either normal or small helpings of healthy food in front of other people, wanting to be seen as 'normal' or 'controlled/anorexic';

☐ feel very distressed about the weight gained as a result of the binges. If you were previously anorexic, or close to it, family and friends will be delighted by this weight gain, seeing it as a sign that you are better. You actually feel worse than ever, having failed to control your appetite and weight. You are not better, but feel unable to tell people what is wrong;

☐ feel totally dominated by your cravings for food, and depressed by your inability to control them;

☐ occasionally become reckless by abusing alcohol or drugs, shoplifting (usually food) or becoming promiscuous.

The physical effects of bulimia include tooth decay, throat infections and gum disease from vomiting, and possible heart and kidney problems from regular purging. Excessive overeating in itself can be potentially fatal because of the sudden stretching of the stomach lining. And being over-weight when young can lead to the onset of diabetes and heart disease in later life.

Other side effects include exhaustion (after bingeing and purging), depression, possible financial problems due to lavish spending on binges, poor concentration, irritability and social isolation. If you have bulimia, you will almost certainly try to hide your feelings of inadequacy and unhappiness by presenting an image of confidence and success.

Many people eat compulsively in secret, but do not purge. Like bulimics, compulsive eaters are addicted to food and, like them, are distressed by their weight and their inability to control their appetite.

Both bulimics and compulsive eaters find food a comfort and a security, as well as a source of unhappiness and fear. This is partly why the cycle of binge-purge-starve, once begun, is so difficult to break. Difficult, but not impossible.

5

Looking for a Way Out

'My arms are sore with scars where I have cut myself to release the pain,' Penny told me. 'People think I want attention, but this is not so. Cutting yourself lets the pain from your mind go to your arm.'

People with eating problems invariably have very low self-esteem. When they manage to control or lose weight by not eating, they begin to feel better about themselves.

Kirsty, whose eating problems began when she was in college, recalls, 'I felt so superior when I wasn't eating, when I had lost weight. I felt I was good at something. I felt like a somebody instead of a non-person.' Anorexics feel good when they are not eating. They believe that their rigid self-control around food and their waif-like appearance give them an identity they wouldn't otherwise have.

But if you are caught up in the bulimia cycle, and find you can no longer starve yourself—indeed you

The binge-purge-binge vicious circle can be broken.

cannot stop eating—you will feel more unhappy and disgusted with yourself than ever before. These intense feelings of despair and self-hatred will often lead a bulimic or compulsive eater to try to blot out her feelings, maybe by self-mutilation, maybe by alcohol or drug abuse.

When Kirsty's starvation regime cracked, she found herself bingeing frequently and putting on weight. She tried to blot out her emotions by slashing her arms with razors. Like Penny, she found that the pain in her arms took her mind off the binge—and what had caused it.

Those who drink alcohol after bingeing or take drugs are also trying to escape from reality. Alcohol and drugs can provide a high that obliterates feelings of shame and insecurity. They can also lull the sufferer into a long, heavy sleep during which she is safe from bingeing and having to think.

But, of course, when the effects wear off the food cravings will still be there—and so will the problems which lie behind them.

Whatever your preferred 'escape route', you might well turn to it when you are making a concerted effort to control your eating. For example, most bulimics have an alternative form of self-abuse for their non-bingeing days.

'I had been trapped in dieting, bingeing and bulimia for about twelve years. I did have trouble-free periods—or did I? I just transferred my obsession on to something else,' recalls Suzanne.

Turning to alcohol, drugs or cigarettes; cutting or burning yourself; becoming promiscuous—these are not the answers to bulimia or compulsive eating. In fact, they could mark the beginning of another addiction.

The problems lying beneath your addiction need to be faced and dealt with before recovery from your eating disorder is possible. But recovery really is possible.

6

The First Step to Recovery

Everyone who has had an eating disorder will have experienced ambivalent feelings about recovery. All anorexics say they want to recover—but they don't want to put on any weight. All bulimics and compulsive eaters would like to eat normally—but first they want to diet to lose their excess weight.

Once you know that you have an eating disorder, you have to choose what, if anything, you are going to do about it. If you choose to recover, these negative feelings will not go away. The battle against an eating disorder is fought in the mind. You will need support, especially for those days when the negative feelings are strongest and you feel like giving up.

Many sufferers, especially bulimics and compulsive eaters, are independent people, totally unused to sharing their feelings with anyone—least of all a psychiatrist or therapist.

Some people try to push their eating problems—

and the underlying ones—to the back of their mind, hoping that will make them go away. It will not. Bingeing will recur until the disorder has been properly dealt with. Because very few sufferers can do this by themselves, finding help is essential.

There are various means of help available for sufferers of eating disorders. These include the medical profession, self-help and support groups, and trained therapists. Although there are millions of sufferers, each person is unique, and what helps one will not necessarily help another. It is worth considering and checking out various types of help and treatment until you find one that is right for you.

Kirsty began to recover from bulimia after seeing a psychiatrist who told her to keep a diary of what she ate and how she felt before, during and after eating. As well as helping to clarify the reasons and feelings behind her binges, Kirsty found that the diary helped her to control her eating because she felt accountable to someone.

Jayne, unlike many other sufferers, found that her second hospital stay helped her to move away from anorexia. The doctors helped her to establish regular food intake and to learn to relax. After that, Jayne's own determination took over. She was further helped by the empathy of other ex-sufferers in a local self-help group.

Suzanne's twelve-year battle with overeating and weight preoccupation began to end when she started to attend local Overeaters Anonymous meetings. Sufferers attending OA meetings follow a Twelve-step Plan, adapted from the steps set out by Alcoholics Anonymous. Suzanne discovered that the twelve steps worked for her as long as she was prepared to work at them.

Following the twelve-step plan, the sufferer admits she is powerless over food and that her life has become unmanageable. She recognizes that only a Power greater than herself can restore her to sanity. The sufferer then turns her will and life over to that Power, asks him to remove defects of character, and states her willingness to make amends to people she has harmed in the past. The eleventh step is to improve conscious contact with that Power by prayer and meditation.

Suzanne, who was a Christian, realized that Jesus Christ was the only Power who could conquer her eating disorder. Day by day, with encouragement from people in her support group, she began turning her eating habits over to him. Regularly she prayed for healing in all areas of her life. As she became aware of relationships that needed mending, she took the initiative and asked for forgiveness.

Suzanne did not see immediate results, but she persisted. Gradually her faith in God grew stronger as her relationships with other people improved and her desire to overeat diminished. Today Suzanne has normal eating habits and is happier than ever before. She credits the power of Jesus Christ for the change in her life.

7

Sharing Your Feelings

Many anorexics are afraid to tell their doctors that they have an eating disorder, fearing they will be sent to hospital. But unless you are extremely under-weight, or so depressed that you might attempt suicide, hospitalization is unlikely. Instead, anorexics will probably be referred to a psychiatrist, psycho-logist or psychotherapist.

Bulimics and compulsive eaters can face a different problem when seeking help.

'My doctor didn't believe I had an eating disorder because I wasn't thin,' remembers Kirsty.

Increased research into eating disorders has helped to make doctors more aware of the problems, however, and bulimics and compulsive eaters should be able to find a therapist through their own doctor.

In the past, hospital treatment of anorexics has proved largely ineffective. Many anorexics would comply with the hospital regime and reach their target weight simply to be discharged quickly and resume their diet. However, there are encouraging signs that this situation is improving. Some hospitals now have special units for people with eating disorders, with psychiatric help available to discover the root of the problem.

Many sufferers have benefited from seeing a psychiatrist or therapist for discussion on a regular basis. Being able to talk about eating problems and what lies behind them can be therapeutic—and these experts are able to suggest alternative, positive ways of coping with life.

Self-help and support groups are currently regarded as one of the best forms of help available to people with eating disorders. Many countries have national organizations that set up and co-ordinate local groups. Meetings are often held on a weekly or twice-monthly basis. Groups are usually run by ex-sufferers, and members are free to talk about their problems and anxieties with people who understand and can offer advice.

Talking to someone who understands eating disorders always comes as a relief to a sufferer, who may well have kept her problems to herself for several years. 'For once I found myself able to talk, discuss and even laugh about my eating habits without feeling weird, dirty or guilty,' recalls one bulimic woman. 'It really helped to be able to talk to someone who completely understood what I was going through.'

There are other forms of help available. Universities and colleges offer advisory services and frequently help people with eating disorders. Many churches provide help of this kind too. Even if these people are not specialists in eating problems, they can still listen, which may be all you need. Or they may be able to refer you to another good source of help.

Whichever form of help or treatment you choose, remember that your recovery basically depends on you. Help is available, but you can only be helped if you are willing to co-operate. No one is going to wave a magic wand and make you better overnight.

8

Putting an End to Anorexia

'It is a battle to eat. I know when I am hungry, but I deny it. And when food is set before me, it makes me feel ill just to look at it. The process of putting food into my mouth and chewing it is alien to me, even though I have done it since I was a small child,' Alison confessed.

An eating disorder is always symptomatic of something else. It is important to find out what lies behind eating disorders and then deal with it. It is equally important to work towards eating normally again.

The longer one suffers with an eating problem, the harder it is going to be to return to eating normally. Habits become deeply ingrained. Old habits and rituals will need to be broken even after the initial cause of the disorder has been put behind you.

Most anorexics long to be able to eat normally, but they want to remain thin. They are afraid that once they start eating, they will never be able to stop—and they will become fat. This doesn't have to happen! It is better to return to normal eating gradually than to risk losing control and bingeing.

The following suggestions from ex-sufferers can help make recovery easier.

☐ Remember that anorexia is your way of coping with life at the moment. Until you develop a

Being able to talk about an eating problem is an important first step to recovery.

positive alternative, the anorexia will not go away.

☐ There is a balance between not eating and over-eating, between being thin and being fat. It is this healthy balance you should aim for.

☐ Don't think recovery means going from eating virtually nothing to immediately tucking into three large meals plus desserts! Build up slowly toward normal eating. Eating one extra piece of fruit or having milk with your cereal can be a large step forward in the early stages of recovery.

☐ Try to eat with other people at normal times, even if you eat very little. If you live alone, try to break away from the fear of going out for meals. Or invite friends round to share a meal with you.

☐ When you go out for a meal, don't panic. Remember, it's just one meal; it's not going to affect the rest of your life.

☐ Try to eat healthy, nutritious food rather than chocolate or cakes. Fruit, vegetables, lean meat, whole-grain bread—these are better for you, especially as your body has been undernourished, and you won't feel so guilty about having eaten them!

☐ If you exercise obsessively, try to cut down slowly as you are building up your food intake.

☐ If you weigh yourself every day, you might find it beneficial to throw the scales out while your body adjusts to more normal eating.

☐ Work on your social skills and assertiveness, so that you lose your fear of involvement with others.

☐ It is important to have someone to talk to when things become too much.

☐ Live one day at a time rather than looking at recovery as a huge, daunting process.

9
Curing Compulsive Eating

People who binge frequently are addicted to food in
the way that some people are addicted to alcohol or
drugs. Addiction to food is not taken as seriously as
alcohol or drug addiction by the medical profession or
by the general public. Perhaps this is because the
health risks are often not as great. However, health
risks such as heart disease and diabetes do exist—and
unlike the alcoholic or drug addict, the compulsive
eater cannot avoid the addictive substance completely. People have to eat food.

As with anorexia, bulimia and overeating actually
serve a purpose in the sufferer's life. They help the
sufferer cope with long-term problems and daily
stress. They also help the sufferer to escape from
reality. After realizing, too late, that I had missed a
question in one of my final exams at university, my
reaction was to buy and eat a large carton of ice cream,
a packet of crisps and a bar of chocolate. Then I was

able to forget about the exam and worry instead about how I was going to burn off the calories.

People who have successfully overcome their addiction to food and overeating have used a number of strategies, particularly in the early days of their recovery. Ex-sufferers advise:

☐ Try to eat three normal meals a day, preferably with other people.

☐ Try to stop purging even though initially it will mean you put on weight. Purging is harmful; if you can stop, you will have broken one part of the binge-purge-starve cycle.

☐ If you have become dependent on laxatives, cut down on the number you take until you have stopped entirely.

☐ Put all thoughts of dieting out of your mind and concentrate on eating normally. Depriving yourself of food one week will inevitably lead to eating too much the next.

☐ If you feel you are about to binge, do something to avoid it. Phone a friend, go for a walk, write a letter. One former bulimic kept a box of suggestions of alternatives to bingeing. Every time she felt like bingeing, she would take out one of the suggestions and do what it said.

☐ If you do binge, put the food on a plate and try to eat it more slowly. Don't allow yourself to eat anything directly from the packet or while you are standing up.

☐ If you have made yourself vomit after bingeing, eat something nutritious right away to break the binge-purge-starve cycle.

☐ When you want to binge, ask yourself what you really want. If you haven't eaten for several hours, you are probably hungry. It is better to eat a nourishing meal than to eat chocolates and cakes. If you are bored or lonely, it is better to go out to visit someone or do something than to stay in and binge.

☐ Identify the foods that trigger a binge. Common-place trigger foods are cereals, bread, dried fruit and chocolate. Avoid them for a while and see if the binges stop. If they do, it may mean you have an allergy to a particular food.

☐ Some people suffer from low blood sugar and glucose intolerance, which makes their bodies physically crave sweet foods. Yeast infections can also cause food cravings, particularly for bread and alcohol. If you suspect you may have low blood sugar or a yeast infection, seek advice from a doctor or a nutritionist who will advise you on foods to eat and foods to avoid.

☐ Identify the situations that cause you to binge. Stress, tiredness, loneliness, boredom, frustration —all these feelings can cause people to overeat. Some people eat to relax or to punish themselves for doing well at something—or for not doing something well enough. Find other ways of coping with these emotions and occasions.

☐ Work at accepting yourself as you are, both physically and mentally.

10

Short-term Triggers

What made you decide to stop eating? Why did you start bingeing? Most sufferers can remember the incident, remark or situation which first triggered their eating disorder.

Kirsty started dieting at college because she wanted to be better than her fellow students at something. Mary lost weight to lose the stolid appearance that she felt made other people depend on her. By being small, she believed, she would be able to start depending on someone else. 'I hoped that by not eating I would become so weak that someone would scoop me into their arms and I could depend on them,' she says.

After keeping my weight deliberately low for four years, I started bingeing in response to unhappiness in my first job and the news that my father was losing his sight.

If an eating disorder is caught during its early

Eating nutritious foods will help the body to recover from an eating disorder.

stages, recovery is easier and quicker than if it is allowed to run its course. In the early stages, the trigger can be identified and dealt with. Eating habits can thus be restored to normal before they become deeply rooted.

Unfortunately, in those early days, sufferers delude themselves that they are in control or can regain control of their eating. When I started bingeing I refused to seek help, believing I could control the urge to eat and return to my low-calorie diet. I was wrong. I was unable to control my eating habits for several years after I had left the job which was making me unhappy and after I had come to terms with my father's blindness.

If you do know exactly what is causing you to diet or binge, try to find the courage to deal with it. Many sufferers have recovered once the trigger was re-moved. If a job, relationship or situation is making you ill, it is worth asking yourself if it is all that important to you.

Many people with eating disorders are employed in particularly stressful jobs. Nurses are especially vulnerable, since working shifts means it is difficult to establish a normal, healthy eating pattern. Women involved in what are traditionally seen as men's jobs also tend to develop unhealthy eating habits, often going home to snack on junk food because they are too tired to make themselves a meal.

Feeling unfulfilled emotionally and mentally is another trigger to an eating disorder. It is important to be able to acknowledge and express your true feelings. It is also important to have interests outside home and work.

But beneath these emotions is a need for spiritual wholeness. When Jayne had recovered from anorexia, she became a Christian. She realized that Jesus Christ could change her life, that he loved her and wanted her to be happy. Having committed her life to him, she found a completeness that she had never before experienced. 'When I came to know Jesus,' she says,

'I knew that the final void had been filled.'

Since her recovery, Jayne has been involved in running self-help groups for sufferers. She has found that those with faith and trust in a loving, caring God have been the ones making the most headway in their recovery.

'They still have problems, but they have an inner peace and knowledge that with time their habits will be washed away,' Jayne explains. 'They have shifted their need for security from food control to the certain security of the love of God.

11
Long-term Causes

While there is always an immediate or short-term trigger for an eating disorder, there are often deep-rooted, long-term problems and unresolved conflicts at the core of the syndrome. Often these have been pushed to the back of the sufferer's mind, replaced by worries about food and weight. The sufferer should be prepared to bring these past hurts and rejections to the surface to deal with them.

Many sufferers, for example, were born prematurely and spent their first days in an incubator. Some psychiatrists believe that this early separation from a mother's love leads a baby to see food as a source of comfort.

Girls who have been adopted often develop eating disorders in their late teens and early twenties, perhaps because they feel they have been rejected by their natural parents. Their lack of roots can lead them to question their identity, which often triggers an eating disorder.

Bad eating patterns throughout childhood invariably lead to trouble later on. Some teenagers who were overweight as children will diet in an attempt to recapture their 'lost' childhood. Other children, who were able to eat what they liked while remaining thin, suddenly will have weight problems when they stop growing upwards and begin growing outwards.

Many sufferers were over-protected during their childhood. They then find themselves unable to cope with the real world when they eventually leave home. Although intelligent and capable, a sufferer will feel ineffectual because she has never been trained to cope with conflicts or relationships in a positive way.

A surprising number of sufferers have been sexually abused in their childhood, which has led to relationship problems later on.

Potential anorexics and bulimics tend to be quiet, serious, studious children, often regarded by adults as very mature for their age. Their perfectionism and the fact that they take themselves and life too seriously often lead to the onset of an eating disorder.

Sufferers often say that they have never really fitted in or belonged anywhere. Their way of coping with this is to withdraw from other people or by presenting an image of confidence and success. By erecting such barriers, they find themselves more cut off than before.

Sufferers can work through the problems of the past by sharing them with a therapist or a friend they trust. The only way you can really come to terms with the past is by forgiving the people who have hurt you. When Jesus was crucified, he forgave his executioners by praying, 'Father, forgive them. They don't know what they are doing.' Of course, this is easier said than done.

It helps to realize that those who hurt us in the past probably did not know the effect of their words or actions. Even if the actions were deliberate, spending our lives resenting and hating people is not going to make the pain go away. The only way we can find peace with ourselves and with God is by forgiving others.

We also need to forgive ourselves. So many people with eating disorders are punishing themselves for failing to live up to their own or others' expectations. We need to learn to accept and love ourselves as we really are so that we can accept and love others.

But how can we forgive others and ourselves? How can we get rid of guilt for our own failures and resentment for the failures of others? There is only one way: by understanding that God loves us so much that he sent his son, Jesus Christ, to die for us.

When Jesus died, he took all of our pain and guilt with him to the grave. When he rose from the dead, it was to offer us new life and complete forgiveness.

When we know we are forgiven, we can stop punishing and hurting ourselves. When we receive God's forgiveness, we can forgive other people with his help.

12
Finding Hope

After spending some eight weeks in hospital being brought up to a normal weight, Sandra spent nearly four months in a psychiatric department to continue her recovery. She regularly attended the psychiatric department, as an outpatient, for two more years.

'When it was suggested that I go into a psychiatric department, my pride was hurt. To think of myself in a "nuthouse"! I wanted to get out and be part of life again,' recalls Sandra. 'Looking back, though, I see how wise a move it was. Although I was putting on weight, my mind had not changed. My attitudes were still the same, and I had a lot of re-learning to do.'

Sandra hated putting on weight. 'All the years I had spent struggling to be the thinnest, all the achievements related to my eating disorder—being noticed, being seen as strong-willed—all this was taken from me.' She found, though, that she enjoyed food, although it took years for her to be able to admit this or to be able to say something as simple as 'I'm hungry'.

As her weight increased, Sandra found she was able to think more clearly and to have interests other than food and calories. But she also found that lots of problems, feelings and anxieties that had been pushed to one side by her anorexia began to come to the surface. She had to learn to deal with these without retreating into anorexia.

While she was in hospital, Sandra became a Christian. 'God,' she says, 'has held me and supported me through the years of recovery, and he is still doing so.' On becoming a Christian, Sandra expected an instant, overnight recovery. 'I thought that if I was a Christian, I should be healed once and for all—no traces of anorexia left in me. It didn't happen like that, and I had to realize that recovery would be a slow and sometimes painful process, with me having responsibility a lot of the time. I could not expect God to do everything for me.'

Sandra, now a language teacher, admits that her thinking is still sometimes influenced by anorexia. 'There are little niggling fears and anxieties and rules that were made long ago that I tend to hold on to and maybe lean on sometimes.' She believes that one day she will be completely free of anorexia; in the meantime, she has found praying and sharing her problems with fellow Christians invaluable.

'Sometimes it's so easy to believe someone is OK once they look human again,' she says. 'But I know that isn't the case. In fact, problems start then! I believe support is needed still, years after physical recovery has taken place. Physical recovery must be followed by expert therapy so that the sufferer's mind is healed and her thinking is straightened out.'

13
Towards Recovery

Having to eat every day is not the only problem facing someone who is struggling to overcome an eating disorder. You will also have to struggle with media and social pressures to be thin.

'Every day you have to look at articles telling you about some wonder diet which will make you lose a stone (fourteen pounds) in a week,' says Mary. 'And every day you have to listen to these tiny little girls talking about going on diets—and you still have to try to eat three normal meals each day.'

Media and social pressures are unlikely to go away, so you just have to get used to them. Coping with them is easier if you can learn to love and accept yourself as you are, not continually compare yourself with other people. Once you have established a normal eating pattern that makes you feel healthy, you will find it easier to ignore articles telling you that you need to lose weight to be happy and successful.

And knowing how much God values you is a tremendous incentive to take good care of yourself.

You also need to learn to handle other people's comments about your weight as you return to normal eating. Most people are very blunt about a person's figure in a way they would not be about anything else. Every ex-anorexic has had to listen to someone telling her that she looks better now that she is fatter!

People who know about your eating problems, while providing welcome support in the early days, may well become a source of frustration later on. Because of your previous deceitful ways with food, people may question any legitimate excuse you may have for not going out for a meal with them. And if you dislike a certain food regarded as fattening—I don't like cream and cheese—people will imagine you are trying to save calories!

You need to learn to be assertive around food as well as in your relationships with other people. Choose what you like from a menu, rather than waiting to see what everyone else is having—and then having something with fewer calories. Although you can learn a lot about normal eating from other people, you shouldn't fall into the trap of eating the same things at the same time as they do.

As you work towards normality, you will often feel you are taking two steps forward and one step back. After a long period of normal eating, you may find yourself bingeing after a particular crisis or longing to be thin again following someone's careless remark. You need to have patience with yourself at these

Recovery will be aided by eating with other people at normal times.

times. Remember that you are making steady improvement and that you will not continue to lapse for ever.

God stands ready to pick us up every time we fall; all we need to do is ask. He will start us down the road again—the road to complete recovery.

14

Life Can Be Good

When you are eating normally again and are no longer plagued by fear of food and the desire to lose weight, you may well want to help sufferers who are in the position you were in.

Many ex-sufferers, like Jayne and Suzanne, run the support groups that they formerly attended. Their experiences, and their methods of coping, help to encourage and motivate other sufferers.

Today people are becoming more aware of eating disorders, and ex-sufferers can help others to understand the problems. Ex-sufferers are the only people who can really know what a person with an eating disorder is going through.

Sometimes, however, ex-sufferers need to forget about their eating problems for a year or so after recovery, while they come to terms with their own disorder. After setting their problems aside for a while, they feel more able to help current sufferers without having constant reminders of their old habits.

Once the eating problems are over, many ex-sufferers are surprised to find how much they can enjoy life again.

'I never dreamed life could be so good,' says Donna, who has been both anorexic and bulimic. 'Eating has a wonderful place in my life now. I eat three meals a day, and I enjoy eating healthy foods. I can enjoy sports again—I go to the gym once a week, go running occasionally and go to body-conditioning classes when I feel like it.'

Sometimes people fear that when a crisis comes along years later, they might, like some ex-alcoholics, lapse back into their eating disorder. However—

☐ if you have completely dealt with the causes of your eating disorder, and

☐ if you have found a positive way to handle life's problems, and

☐ if you have learned to look to Jesus Christ, and not yourself, for power to change—
there is no reason why you should ever need an eating disorder to protect yourself from life again.